NATIONAL GEOGRAPHIC

Ladders

Watery World

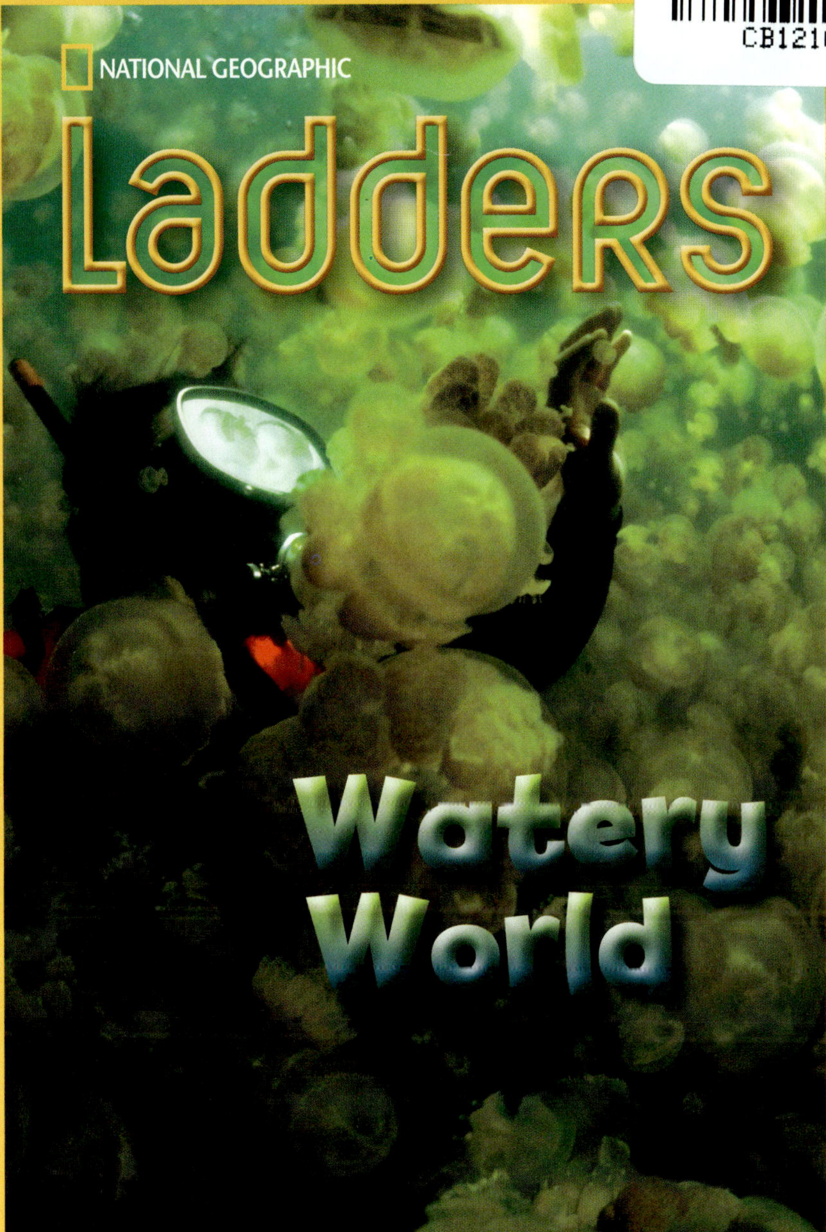

GENRE Science Article

Read to find out about two very different ocean creatures.

Creatures of the DEEP

by Trudie O'Brien

Every sea animal has its place in the ocean's majestic and watery world. Yet the whale and the octopus are particularly interesting. Tails, blowholes, flukes, and migration in pods make whales of any **species** fascinating to study. Octopuses are an underwater spectacle with eight arms, suckers, ink jets, and camouflage techniques.

Species of both creatures vary in size. The blue whale, however, is the largest animal on the planet.

Octopuses range from very small to very large. One species can fit in a human hand. Another species is bigger than an adult human. Whales and octopuses live in similar environments of the ocean, but they are different in many ways. They have different life spans. They have differences in the way they look and behave. Dive into the water and get a close-up look at these two amazing creatures!

This humpback whale swims near the ocean's surface.

Octopuses, like this giant Pacific octopus, are mollusks. A mollusk is a soft-bodied animal without an internal skeleton.

Ocean Giants

Whales migrate seasonally from one part of the ocean to another part. They travel in a group, or pod, with a calf or with several other adult whales and calves. Scientists try to follow whales on their **marine** migrations, as this is often their best opportunity to learn about each species. How do whales know the route to their annual ocean breeding or feeding waters? What abilities do young calves have? How do whale parents help their offspring? Scientists try to find answers to these questions. Scientists track whales to learn about their life cycles in the wild.

Humpbacks in the same area make the same song-like sounds within a season. The songs change from season to season.

Blue whales have a streamlined body shape with a broad, flat front part.

All whales communicate with sounds. Whales are one of the loudest animal species on the planet. Humans don't often hear their underwater noises. Humpback whales make song-like, musical sounds. Their songs are communications, but scientists haven't fully unlocked their messages.

Scientists also work to make sure certain species of whale will stay alive for a long time. Blue whales and humpback whales are two endangered whale species. Their populations have decreased, but hopefully with help these species can increase their numbers.

Whale Size Up

blue whale
Length: 25 to 32 meters (85 to 105 feet)
Weight: up to 181 metric tons (200 tons)

humpback
Length: 14.6 to 19 meters (48 to 62.5 feet)
Weight: about 36 metric tons (40 tons)

gray whale
Length: 12.2 to 15.3 meters (40 to 50 feet)
Weight: 14.5 to 36 metric tons (30 to 40 tons)

bus
Length: about 11 meters (36 feet)
Weight: 9.75 metric tons (10.75 tons)

1 metric ton = 2,204.6 pounds
1 standard ton = 2,000 pounds

Gray whales are covered with barnacles and other organisms.

The Ocean's Mammal

How can an air-breathing **mammal** live in the ocean? A whale is a mammal that breathes air through one or two blowholes on top of its head. Above water, the whale draws a huge breath, closes the blowhole, then dives down. It holds its breath under water, swimming and feeding for about 10 or 15 minutes. When it comes to the surface for air, it opens its blowhole and exhales. The air it blows out can shoot water as high as 9.1 meters (30 feet). Whales may dive very deep, but they usually swim near the surface, where they can come up for air.

Blue, humpback, and gray whales cannot bite or chew. They are **baleen** whales. This means they have comb-like structures called baleen instead of teeth. The baleen is plates of fingernail-like material on a whale's upper jaws. Baleen plates have bristles that act like a strainer.

To feed, a blue or humpback whale gulps a huge mouthful of water containing tiny animals. Its tongue forces the water through the baleen. This filters out thousands of miniature creatures, including krill, a shrimp-like animal, that whales then swallow. The bottom-feeding gray whale doesn't gulp mouthfuls of water. It takes in both water and mud, and strains out the tiny shellfish that live in the mud.

Whales have a tail with wide flukes, or flattened pads that fan out sideways. To swim, strong muscles move the flukes up and down, pushing the whale forward. The huge tail helps the whale navigate. Whale migration journeys vary, but gray whales swim 20,000 kilometers (12,430 miles) round-trip from summer waters to warmer waters in winter.

Whales use group cooperation. Humpback whales have been known to work together to gather fish for feeding and to fend off killer sharks.

The cream colored baleen helps this whale feed on tiny krill in ocean water.

Whales breathe through a blowhole.

Unlike fish tails, whale flukes fan out sideways.

Female whales give birth to one calf at a time. Calves continue to grow and develop for about ten years.

Unusual Mollusks

Octopuses, like slugs or snails, are **mollusks** and **invertebrates.** They do not have skeletons or a backbone. Octopuses have arms, sometimes mistakenly called tentacles. An octopus's arm has suckers along it. Squid have both arms and tentacles. A tentacle has suckers at the end point, sometimes called hooks or rings.

Octopuses live between crevices in rocks and coral. Their soft bodies allow them to squeeze in tight spaces, away from predators and in position to make attacks. They are also able to change color and texture to camouflage themselves.

Whales may live as long as 80 years or more, but octopuses have a much shorter life span. Giant Pacific octopuses live for up to five years. The much smaller common octopus lives between one and two years. Male octopuses die after mating. When female octopuses lay eggs, they stop eating to watch over the eggs. After the eggs hatch, the female octopuses die.

The giant Pacific octopus is the largest octopus species. It can be larger than a human. Many other octopuses are small enough to fit on a spoon. The common octopus species is somewhat in between. Average sizes are about half a meter (1.6 feet).

Giant Pacific octopuses move between shallow waters to depths of 1,500 meters (4,921 feet).

Common octopuses will sometimes collect objects to create gardens or fortresses around their lairs.

Octopus Size Up

bus
Length: about 11 meters (36 feet)
Weight: 9.75 metric tons (10.75 tons)

giant Pacific octopus
Length: 3 to 5 meters (9.75 to 16 feet)
Weight: 10 to 50 kilograms (22 to 110 pounds)

common octopus
Length: 30.5 to 91.4 centimeters (12 to 36 inches)
Weight: 3 to 10 kilograms (6.6 to 22 pounds)

Many octopus species hatch and begin their life cycles as tiny larvae. They swim to the surface and start their lives as plankton.

An octopus's ink is a mixture of dark fluid and mucus. This giant Pacific octopus was swimming in waters near British Columbia, Canada.

An octopus can change its color or texture to blend in with its surroundings.

Octopuses: Escape and Attack

Octopuses have heads with large eyes and beak-like mouths. Suckers on their eight arms have sense organs, which feel, smell, and taste. An octopus looks very unusual, but you could snorkel right by one and miss it. This master of camouflage can hide in plain sight. Its skin has cells that can change color and can make the octopus match the colors and patterns around it. Special muscles in the skin can change its texture to blend in with pebbly or smooth surroundings.

If a predator spots an octopus, the octopus shoots a blast of water from its siphon, or funnel. The force of the water thrusts the octopus forward like a jet engine. The octopus hides its escape by spraying black ink. If escape proves difficult, the octopus can shed an arm to keep the predator happy while the octopus jets away. Later the octopus regrows the arm.

The common octopus and the giant Pacific octopus dwell in moderately warm ocean waters. The giant Pacific octopus can be found in the Pacific Ocean near North America, the Aleutian Islands, and Japan.

Like whales, octopuses are very intelligent; they are the most intelligent animals without backbones. Their arms allow them to show their intelligence in ways that whales cannot. For example, they can open jars and solve mazes in lab tests.

Variation within each species of whale or octopus makes these ocean animals even more interesting. Octopuses have inherited traits that allow them to quickly act and react in their habitat. Whales feed, migrate, and breed, repeating this pattern for many years. Scientists study the habits of these two amazing ocean creatures and work hard to protect their populations.

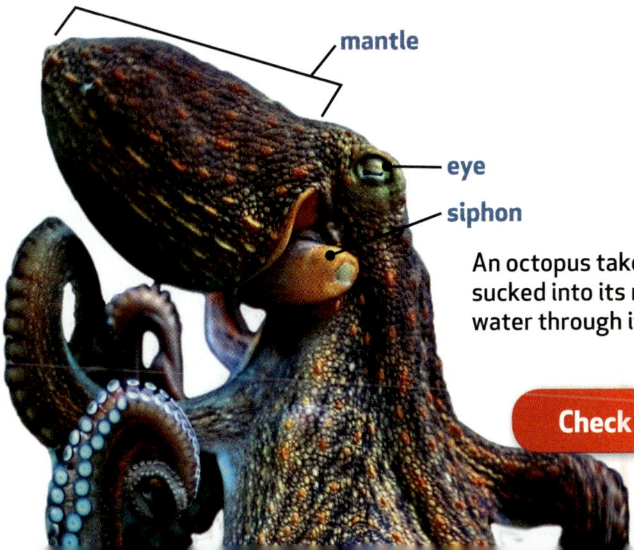

An octopus takes oxygen from water sucked into its mantle. It expels the water through its siphon.

Check In What amazes you about whales and octopuses?

GENRE Fantasy

Read to find out how one octopus learns to escape ocean predators.

Sea Warrior

by Hilary Wagner
illustrated by Denis Zilber

Murdina jolted at the sight of a young blue whale barreling toward her, his huge mouth wide open for krill. Shivering, she dashed into the shadows of some nearby coral. Her eldest sister had told her a blue whale would never eat an octopus, but even so, Murdina worried it might just snatch her up by accident. Even the blue whale pups were enormous! Creeping out of the shadows after the whale passed by, Murdina sighed. Her name meant sea warrior, but she felt more like a sea coward.

Predator—she didn't even like the sound of the word. It scared her, but her sister said there are predators lurking everywhere in the depths of the ocean, and an octopus must learn to take care of herself. But she still hadn't mastered the art of camouflage and of changing shapes. She was certain she was the worst pupil in her class. Her teacher explained that her **instincts,** such as camouflage and shape shifting, would kick in when she needed them most. He also said her talents would develop quickly after that, but Murdina wasn't convinced. Her sister said she would learn when she was ready, that her skills would come in time, but what if they didn't come soon enough?

Murdina thought she was hopeless because unlike other octopuses, she was unable to change color and shape, alter the texture of her skin, or escape in a thick cloud of ink. Her **species** could do miraculous things, but it didn't seem she could. She bowed her head sadly and started back for home, knowing her family could protect her. She wanted to be alone with her thoughts, but being alone was too perilous for an inexperienced octopus such as she. Abruptly, Murdina felt a cold rush of water behind her. Her heart racing, she turned to see a hammerhead shark, a fearsome predator, swim through a cloud of silt. At first, she froze. "Conceal yourself!" she whispered, eyes darting everywhere.

Murdina spotted a large rock, latched onto it, and wrapped her arms one by one around its smooth exterior. Nervously, she locked her eyes on its surface, concentrating on its many shades of gray. Within seconds, each brown arm drained of its tawny color, and miniature gray and cream dots sprung up all over her body. She watched as her octopus form vanished before her and what used to be her body was now a perfect match to the rock. The hammerhead sailed just over her head, lazily glanced down at her, and moved on.

"It worked!" Murdina exclaimed, watching the shark swim away. Her teacher had told her that her instincts would kick in when she needed them most. Maybe being so afraid had done the trick, forcing her to take action. Murdina headed for home, excited to tell her sister that her camouflage finally worked.

Nearing home, the sea grew unexpectedly dark. Looking up, Murdina saw an enormous vessel over her head. "A ship!" she said, with a gasp. Her teacher had warned the class to stay far away from ships, especially fishing ships that might be hunting octopuses.

Before she knew it, Murdina was moving up towards the surface at a rapid pace. She realized she'd been caught in a net, and was headed straight towards the fishing boat! The net had holes in it, too small for a full-grown octopus to escape, but maybe she could wriggle out. She tried desperately to squish through a hole, but with no luck. Almost unconsciously, she forced a jet of water through her funnel. Her sister had told her it would give her great speed if she needed it. Instantly, Murdina's body burst through the hole in the net, freeing her. She swam quickly, distancing herself as far away from the ship as possible.

Exhilaration surged through Murdina. Her sister would be proud. She did indeed have octopus instincts. She spun in a circle, her eight arms rippling in the water. She was smiling contentedly when she heard a low voice behind her. "Why so happy, young one?" asked the slithery voice. "What sort of joyous occasion is such a succulent octopus celebrating?"

Anxiously, Murdina turned to find herself face to face with a moray eel. It curled its slick body around her, its sharp teeth gleaming. "Don't be afraid," it said. "I don't want to hurt you." An oily grin spread across its pointed face.

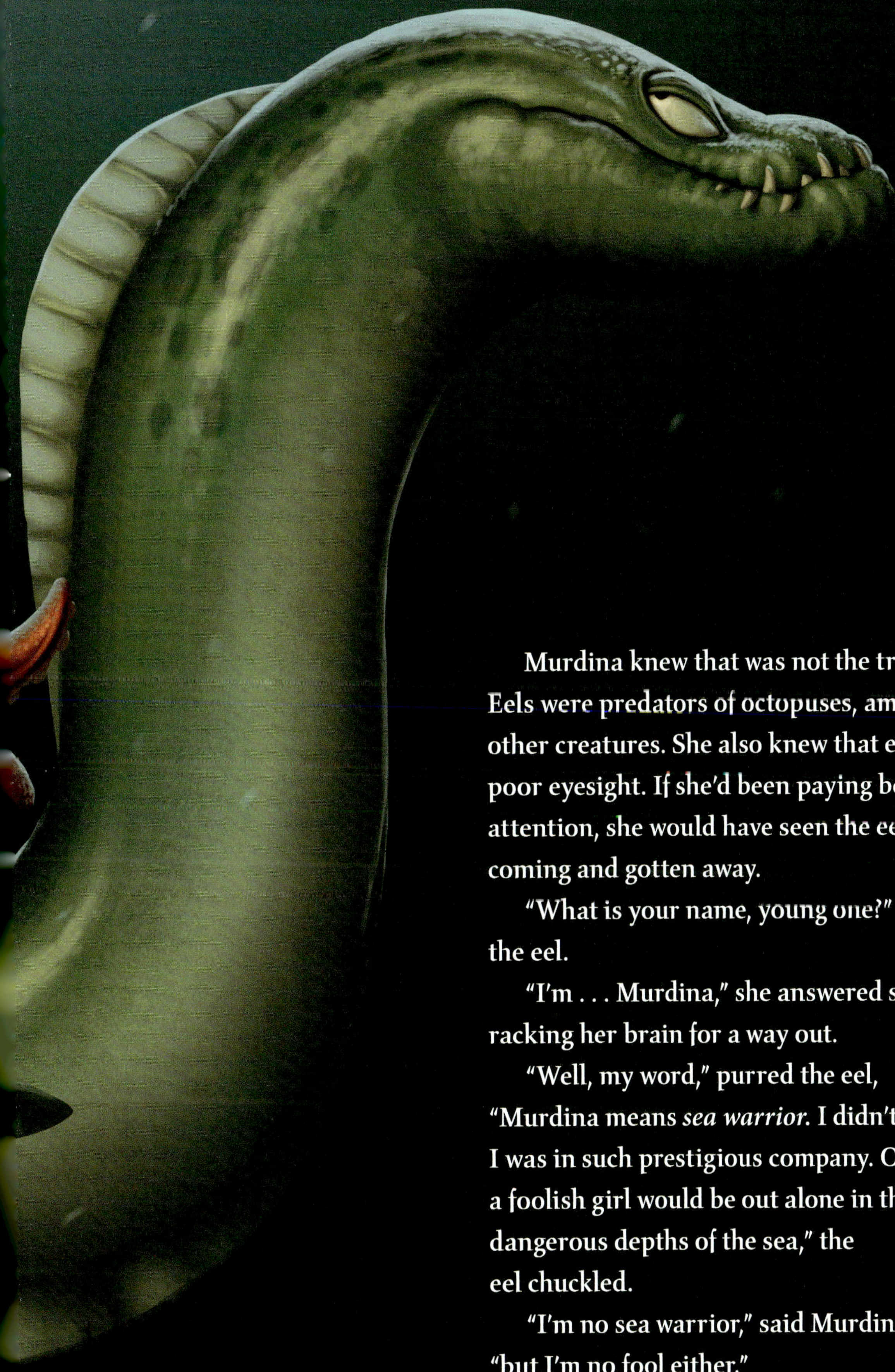

Murdina knew that was not the truth. Eels were predators of octopuses, among other creatures. She also knew that eels had poor eyesight. If she'd been paying better attention, she would have seen the eel coming and gotten away.

"What is your name, young one?" asked the eel.

"I'm . . . Murdina," she answered slowly, racking her brain for a way out.

"Well, my word," purred the eel, "Murdina means *sea warrior.* I didn't know I was in such prestigious company. Only a foolish girl would be out alone in the dangerous depths of the sea," the eel chuckled.

"I'm no sea warrior," said Murdina, "but I'm no fool either."

Eyeing a sea plant, Murdina had an idea. With all her might, she pushed a jet of ink into the eel's face. Soaring through the black cloud of ink, she sailed out of sight and quickly latched onto the base of the ruffled red kelp. In a flash, her skin changed to red, the exact color of the kelp. She shrunk her body down and crimped her arms to look like the kelp's long, frilly blades. The eel swam about in a frenzied circle as it glided by her, completely unaware that Murdina was veiled in the kelp. "Where did you go?" it called out crossly.

Enraged, the eel finally gave up looking for her and swam away. Murdina looked all around, now aware she should save her merriment until she was secure at home. Predators were everywhere. No wonder the octopuses had developed such astounding skills. Murdina kept up her guard and finally arrived at their **marine** burrow. Greeting Murdina, her older sister looked at her curiously. "Something's changed about you," she said. "You look so confident, as though you're a great warrior returning from battle."

"Let's go inside," said Murdina, eyeing her surroundings for predators. "I'll tell you all about it."

Check In What animal behaviors saved Murdina from ocean predators?

GENRE Fantasy **Read to find out** about Charlie's favorite marine animal.

Charlie's Swim

by Hilary Wagner
illustrated by Paule Trudel Bellemare

Rubbing his eyes wearily, Charlie rolled out of bed and walked to the window of the hotel room. He looked out at the ocean, watching it dance up and down the shoreline. He'd been waiting for this day—his twelfth birthday. For his present, his older brother Seth was taking him blue whale watching. Charlie had been studying them in school, and now he'd finally get to see real blue whales, not just pictures of the **species** he'd seen in books and online. He was relieved Seth had agreed. After all, how could he become a **marine biologist** if he only saw blue whales in photographs?

The blue whale is the largest living creature on Earth, with a life span of about 80 years. With a life span that long, Charlie could only imagine how many blue whales lived in the depths of the sea. Weighing a whopping 200 tons, the size of a blue whale was staggering, but then again, the sea was so vast, maybe even the blue whale felt miniscule in it. Softly, he opened the sliding glass door, crept off the patio, and onto the sand. The tiny sand particles stuck to his feet. The sound of the ocean gently hitting the shore was like a rhythmic lullaby. It reminded him of his mother singing to him when he was a child. He wondered if young whales liked the sound, too.

As Charlie watched the frothy waves, a sound filled the air, blaring from the depths of the ocean. It sounded like a tuba, only lower in pitch and much, much louder. It was the call of the blue whale! Charlie sprinted towards the water's edge, the waves just reaching his toes. He knew he shouldn't travel this far out on his own, but something told him he'd be fine. He took a step farther into the water, the cuffs of his pajama pants quickly soaked through. He saw something gliding through the water, the top of its rounded body just breaking the water's surface.

The massive creature in the water called out to him. "Come in the water with me, Charlie," it said, in a boy's voice. "Take a swim with me . . . for your birthday."

Eyes widening, Charlie made out the creature, a young blue whale. "I can't come with you," he called back, hands cupped around his mouth, "I'll drown."

"I promise, you'll be well protected," called the blue whale.

Before Charlie could answer, something odd happened. He looked down at his body, now fully in the water. His body had transformed from a human being into a whale.

Instinctively, Charlie dove after the other blue whale, feeling the cool water rushing around his newly-formed fins and tail. "Wait for me!" he called catching up to the whale. "What's your name?"

"I'm Azul," said the whale, slowing down.

"Where are you headed, Azul?" asked Charlie, his eyes widening at his new acquaintance.

"My parents said it's time to go to the **Costa Rica Dome**," Azul replied. With a slight turn of his head, Charlie spotted two fully-grown blue whales trailing them in the distance. "This is my first winter there; the water stays warmer than near California, and my older brothers say the water is rich with krill."

"I know what krill is," said Charlie, "I read all about it. It's the miniature shrimp-like animal you eat."

Azul bellowed with laughter. "Well, you eat it too, for now, Charlie!"

"How do you eat krill without having any teeth?" asked Charlie, thinking it must be problematic.

"Watch and learn," said Azul, taking a huge mouthful of water and blowing it back out again with great force. "I have a baleen. It helps get rid of the water and keeps every delicious krill. You try it now."

Charlie filled his mouth with water and then pushed it out again, the tiny whiskers in his mouth catching thousands of krill. It tasted especially briny and a little fishy, not something he was used to. He didn't really like it, deciding sandwiches tasted far better.

Charlie noticed something gray and bumpy along the edges of Azul's thick flippers. "What are those little lumps on your flippers? Are they part of your skin?"

Azul glanced at the tips of his flippers. "Oh, those are just barnacles," he replied. "My older brothers told me they hitch rides on whales and other sea creatures sometimes."

"Do the barnacles hurt at all?" asked Charlie, examining their coarse exterior.

"No, and I can knock them off any time I feel like it, but they don't really bother me."

"How much farther away is the Dome?" asked Charlie.

"The water feels much warmer than it did yesterday," said Azul, "so our journey should be ending soon."

"Won't you miss your older brothers in the California waters?" asked Charlie, thinking how much he'd miss Seth if he couldn't see him for an entire winter.

Twisting around, Azul pointed with his massive snout. Charlie's mouth dropped open as he gazed upon a whole pod of young blue whales, traveling behind Azul's parents. "They've all come with you?" he asked in disbelief.

"My parents said they've got a big surprise for us, so this year we all decided to travel to the Dome together," said Azul, "and traveling as a pod, or group, protects us from the orcas too—sometimes they attack the younger whales. Dad always says there is safety in numbers when it comes to predators."

It was hard to believe that the largest creature in the sea could be at risk from predators of any kind, but after today, Charlie supposed anything was possible.

After finally reaching the dome, Azul and Charlie, both terribly hungry, went swimming for krill. Upon their return, all of Azul's brothers had gathered around their parents. "What's going on?" asked Azul, sensing excitement. Within moments, a small blue body soared past him, breaking the water's surface and taking a big breath of air. Azul sailed after the creature, along with the rest of his pod.

Reaching the surface, Azul came upon a small calf, and gazed at her thoughtfully. "Azul," said his father, patting the calf with his flipper, "this is your new sister."

Azul, no longer the youngest in his family, nuzzled up against his only sister. Missing his brother, Charlie suddenly felt very alone.

Charlie awoke to the feeling of gentle nudging against his arm. "Charlie, it's time to wake up." He sat up in bed, finally focusing on Seth, who smiled at him with bleary eyes. "Hey, little brother, it's your birthday, time to get up and see the whales," said Seth, drinking his coffee.

Everything had seemed so authentic, thought Charlie, remembering how it felt to be a whale, swimming in the ocean depths with Azul and his family. For a moment, he was sad, realizing it was only a dream.

Seth ruffled Charlie's hair. "You sure slept late for a budding marine biologist so eager to meet the whales."

Thinking back on the dream, Charlie smiled at his brother.

"Oh, I'm ready to see them," Charlie said, but he already felt like he knew them pretty well.

Check In What surprise did Azul's parents have for him?

Discuss Compare and Contrast

1. What connections can you make between the three pieces in *Watery World*? How are the pieces related?

2. Compare and contrast the two stories, "Sea Warrior" and "Charlie's Swim."

3. How are the topics of the two stories alike and different?

4. What information did you learn about the size of whales and octopuses? Compare the two animals.

5. What questions do you still have about animal life in the ocean?